Breaking Clouds

Christian Poetry

David LaChapelle

Now concerning how and when all this will happen, dear brothers and sisters, we don't really need to write you. For you know quite well that the day of the Lord's return will come unexpectedly, like a thief in the night. When people are saying, "Everything is peaceful and secure," then disaster will fall on them as suddenly as a pregnant woman's labor pains begin. And there will be no escape. ...

1 Thessalonians 5: 1-3 (New Living Translation)

ISBN: 9798369903865

POEMS

[16] For the Lord himself will come down from heaven, with a loud command, with the voice of the archangel and with the trumpet call of God, and the dead in Christ will rise first. [17] After that, we who are still alive and are left will be caught up together with them in the clouds to meet the Lord in the air. And so we will be with the Lord forever. [18] Therefore encourage one another with these words.

1 Thessalonians 4: 16-18 (New International Version)

Preparation

There will come a time

When I will struggle no more

To have my way with the Lord

He will have all of me

That is for sure

From the pain of this world

I hope I will be restored

In that strong direction

A force of winds

I will no longer twist

I cannot resist

It is a waste of time

It must run its course

You hear my plea

I better get in shape

Anticipation

You are hiding Lord

That means the time is near

For your return

To save us from here

We will be made new

We will be with you

My brothers and sisters

A warm embrace

A feast to celebrate

Rewards are in your hands

If I have done wrong

Forgive me

I am not alone

<u>Hope</u>

These are the days we are in

There is no use fighting the moment

Overwhelmed by the state of affairs

That has come to see the light

Shining through the darkest clouds

The anticipation is a lot to take in

Everybody it seems just wants to fly away

To another space

To another place

Go to the Word

Is the only out

Heaven's calling

Hope restored

An Opening

He will light our way

To see the open roads

Carve a clearing in the forest

To make our paths known

This is where it all begins

What I am about to witness

To be part of something splendid

It will all be the norm

Until the morning light arrives

I will wait with surprise

And hold on to His promises forevermore

Straightened

You have earned your wages

Put in your time

You have experience

You have been through the mill

Through all the trials and lies

No one needs to tell you

You can see clearly now

As the noonday sun

Walking in love

To the front door

It has always been there

You did not know the zip code

<u>Amazing</u>

The world is a setting sun

Overlooking a pristine lake

A new horizon dawns

The Lord is in the clouds

His love breaking through

Calling us home

Fear melts away

On that special day

Love is here to stay

To appreciate the beauty without pride

The glory and the ride

A forever romance in eternity

Is about to tide

My Way

I have been trying to fight on my own

For fear of the unknown

I need direction

I need discretion

Forgive me Lord,

For what I am trying to prove

Cannot chart my own course

You will not take me by force

I invite you to release me;

To freedom and liberty

It is a battle waging inside

I will try not to hide

Thank you for your correction

Enabling me to see

What was restricting me

Meaning

You give purpose

A reason to celebrate

I can breathe

That is enough for me

I am grateful for the calling

Your love

The true meaning of above

To know one day,

I will be with you

Words cannot describe

They do no justice to what is real

Although there is so much more

Just bless me Lord

I am all yours

Faith

Want an opportunity

To leave everything behind

At a crossroads

The decision is mine

Not looking back

I am equipped for the task at hand

That I have yet to see

How else can I be

I am locked in your grace

I will see you face to face

Beyond what is near

There is nothing to fear

I have got nothing in the tank

I have got nothing in the bank

I am ready as I will ever be

You are preparing me

To take a leap of faith

I am so inadequate

Moving forward

In your direction

Steady on me feet

You will not let me go

There is nothing to hold on to

But you

Rescued

Looking forward to the sunshine

Where I do not run and hide

From the elements outside

What a sight to see

The Lord has rescued me

A testimony of His love

To bring others to wholeness

No sun screen necessary

The elements are friendly

The clouds have separated

Everywhere is celebration

What a sight to see

The Lord has rescued me

The breaking brought me whole

I thought I would not make it home

What a sight to see

The Lord has rescued me

I like feeling this way

I do not like being dismayed

I do not hold you responsible anymore

To what I was holding onto

Feelings come and go

Putting on a show

I am walking out the door

What a sight to see

The Lord has rescued me

Liberty

Committed

I do not have to know,

Your plans for my life

I do not have to know your will,

Ahead of time

I trust you.

In whatever you may do

I belong to the one who created it all

The source of love forevermore

Healing is in my life

I becoming a new man

I am making a stand

Turned

The past three years:

I read your Word

Studied your heart

You took me through

Did I start this all on my own

Or did I have help in the unknown

Are you with me?

Do you know where I am coming from

All I did was change directions

And the world reflected my intentions

To be so connected

To this loving God

Is something special

I am blessed

I rest

New View

You are real to me

Everything seems so unique

Always looking on the horizon

For the setting of the sun

To finally be complete

End this losing streak

In a battle I cannot seem to win

Never intended on my own

Not my responsibility

The war within

Hope is all we have got

Promise of a better day

All is not lost

Eternity

Glory

God's Love

The pandemic is God's judgment

To change our focus beyond the surface

There is nowhere to hide

The light is shining through the skies

Shifting things around for the final move

Do not be scared

Get in the groove

Come to Him

He will accept you

Bruised and broken,

Is His speciality

Loving you for eternity

In Sync

I just want to feel whole

I just want to be complete

Stable and Secure

Steady on my feet

But you love me more than that

Than to let me have my way

Drawing me closer

To your heartbeat

This is where freedom is found

In a loving relationship

To the one who holds it all

There is nothing more to say

Enough

Hope is not enough

For all my stuff

I need a Savior

Who knows me inside out

To walk with me

Step by step

Through the ups and downs

And greater depths

There is so much going on

It is easy to get lost

And lose my course

Keep me on track

And blow the horn

A Showing

You are pruning me

You are grooming me

From the inside

You will provide

To bear fruit

Abide in the vine

Without you I can do nothing

I need you for everything

For life and fellowship

And so much more

My life depends on you

Being first place in my heart

Because that is who you are

Give me a sign Lord

That everything is going to be okay

That you are working on my behalf

That you are restoring my faith

Show me your loving kindness

In a new way

Give me favor for the day

So, I can keep my fears at bay

Guidance

Paint the lines in the road

So, I do not stray off course

Show me a signal or two

To know your coming through

I need to know your plan

To be a better man

To have something to celebrate

More than living day to day

You do not have to tell me it all

Just show me a little more

Honk if I have gone too far

Just show me a little more

Rewards

Tell me your plan

I cannot make another stand

The way I am

It is too much for this man

I need an open door

I am ready for more

You know what you are doing

I do not have to out do you

I cannot wait any longer

Take my burdens on your shoulders

Set me free

To the next level of being

<u>Looking</u>

I am so inadequate

I want to throw a fit

Why did you make me like this

I feel like closing my fist

It hurts to be so dependent

On something I cannot see

I know you are there

The world tries to disagree

But your fingerprints are everywhere

Just tribulations have blinded me

To see your love in everything

You have opened my eyes

To see what is in disguise

Your light colors my life

To see more than strife

Moving On

I am scared to move on

I am beginning to think this is the norm

I cannot fear what I do not know

You are doing something new

The past cannot repeat

I cannot live in defeat

I must muster up the courage

To face another day

I hope you are with me

To show me your loving grace

Reality

The truth is clear to see

Politics veil has been revealed

There is no hiding anymore

Everything is out in the open

Brought into the light

Exposing the lies to the surface

In the sight of those who believe

We know better

We care to dream

There is no stopping prophecy

It is written in the book

Those who deny the Lord

Will see their destiny on that glorious day

It does not have to be this way

I pray for the lost everyday

Come to the Lord

This is serious business

It is for forever

Your placement

Your new beginning

Graced

The Lord is near

There is nothing to fear

Whatever comes my way

I will be okay

I trust you Lord

For the open door

To make my way to you

You will walk me through

Eternity is calling

I am falling,

Into your loving grace

Forevermore

Stepping Out

You took me through

The valley down low

You held my hand

You walked with me

To open the new

Never letting go

I will spread my wings

And see how my life changes

Giving up my traditions

The lies are past me

Truth shines bright

Your love in me cannot hide

I am stepping out

<u>Becoming</u>

Heaven is calling

A door is swinging open

Walk on through

Love will impress you

A calling of light

A calling so bright

There is nothing to fear

Cannot look back in tears

I feel whole and complete

No sadness or defeat

Less of me

Is liberating

More of you

Is celebrating

Goodness

Things are looking up

I feel the tide is turning

Waves of something good

A beach with hidden treasures

The weather is favorable

For any activity:

That blesses hope

The clouds are disagreeing

The heaviness is good

The light is making a clearing

My burdens burn bright

Fears dissipate into the night

Anxiety left me for now

I feel good

A signpost

Love Me

My labor is not in vain

What you sow you reap

I have forgiven

I have prayed

I have read the Bible

I am at the end

Of striving to send the good

To the win this race

You have set course

I feel a burden lifted

You are carrying me

I am sifted

Rubbish removed

I can now serve

I will be your trophy

Expressions

The clouds are breaking

The sun is singing

Something has happened

Your glory

Things have turned around

I am not scared

There is hope

I was downcast

Now there is an opening

That no man can shut

They can just watch

And see victory take its discourse

New Day

Trials may come

But I see the sun

I feel its warmth

Calling me forth

To be whom I am meant to be

Alert to surprise and blessings

This is where I belong

United with liberty

It was not what I thought it would be

Something better has arrived

I let go and do not hide

Freedom in love

Is where I want to stay

There is more to life

Then being kept at bay

Hold On

You are everything to me

My whole life's meaning

I do not know what to say

I need you to need me

I am trying the best I can

Your way is to make me a better man

You know the way

To come back to you

And not be lost

In this world

There is so much going on

I hold tightly onto you

The Light

Waiting for the sun

To melt the snow

Around my heart

Surrounding my life

Independence from fears

A testimony of tears

To see others for who they are

Keeping score, no more

Searching for love

It is right in front of their nose

We all need a Savior

Jesus is the Lord

Redemption

Great are you Lord

For what you have in store

For those who believe in your name

To live with for eternity

What better way to say

Loving us forevermore

A trophy of your grace

To point others

That you are real

To seal the deal

Redeeming mankind

To his rightful place

Right by your side

Newness

The world is passing by

People are not what they seem

Reality is relative

God's truth is evident

All around this town

People are not the same

I look to the open sky

I see Him with my eye

Cannot be distracted anymore

The Lord is at my door

Correctness

What is good is bad

What is bad is good

Blurred lines

The lies take center stage

The show is on

Let them perform

We know the routine

Nothing can separate

We are on the winning team

We take our rightful place

to Heaven's gate

Acceptance

Worthy is the lamb

Who has forgiven your sins

Into the ocean of His forgetfulness

He remembers them no more

Viewing us through the Father's love

He does not see our flaws

But has compassion on us

That we are made in His image

To show us the way

To a better day

Where we will reside

In the light

And not hide

And bask in His love

Like a plant in the sun

Life will meet us there

And we will fully know

What it is to be known

Forever

You have my attention

I am ready for your descent

I accept your intention

To be with you forever

What a wonderful way

To live the rest of my days

Full of your love

In harmony

In paradise

Forever, and ever and ever and ever and ever

ABOUT THE AUTHOR

David LaChapelle is a born-again Christian living with Paranoid Schizophrenia since the year 2000. David has earned himself two Computer Technical Diplomas from Seneca College in Toronto, Canada in 1994 and 1996. He graduated with a Psychology degree in 2011 from Trent University in Peterborough, Canada where he now calls home. David lives a quiet life and enjoys writing and being an author. He is proud of his works and hopes it will bring him recognition in this life and rewards hereafter. David is a firm believer in reading the Word of God and the power of prayer and wishes the best for all humanity waiting for the Lord's return.

OTHER BOOKS BY DAVID LACHAPELLE

David's Adventure with Schizophrenia: My Road to Recovery

David's Journey with Schizophrenia: Insight into Recovery

David's Victory Thru Schizophrenia: Healing Awareness

David's Poems: A Poetry Collection

1000 Canadian Expressions and Meanings: EH!

Freedom in Jesus

Canadian Slang Sayings and Meanings: Eh!

The Biggest Collection of Canadian Slang: Eh!

Healing Hidden Emotions for Believers

All books and e-books available at Amazon

Manufactured by Amazon.ca
Bolton, ON

31184241R00026